D1142153

A

GIFT BOOK

OF

Roses

TO

.... *IAIN* ....

FROM

.... *EWAN* ....

Accept this.

GIFT BOOK

OF

Roses

Compiled by Bronwyn Hilton

LANSDOWNE

$\mathcal{C}$ONTENTS

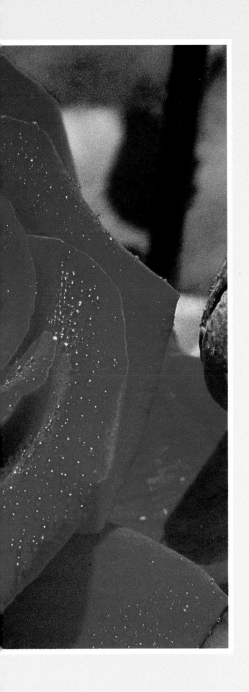

Consider the Rose

Perhaps few people have ever asked themselves why they admire a rose so much more than all other flowers. If they consider, they will find first, that red is, in a delicate graduated state, the lovliest of all pure colours; and secondly, that in the rose there is *no shadow*, except which is composed of colour. All its shadows are fuller in colour than its lights, owing to the translucency and reflective power of its leaves.

JOHN RUSKIN
(1819–1900)
Modern Painters

Ring a ring o' roses, A pocket full of posies, A-tishoo, a-tishoo, We all fall down.

Lilies are white, Rosemary's green;

When you are king I will be queen.

Roses are red, Lavender's blue;

If you will have me, I will have you.

ANON

ROSES OF RHYMES:
RHYMES OF ROSES

The Rose is red, the Rose is white,

The Rose is in my Garden,

I would not part with my sweetheart,

For tuppence ha'penny farden.

ANON

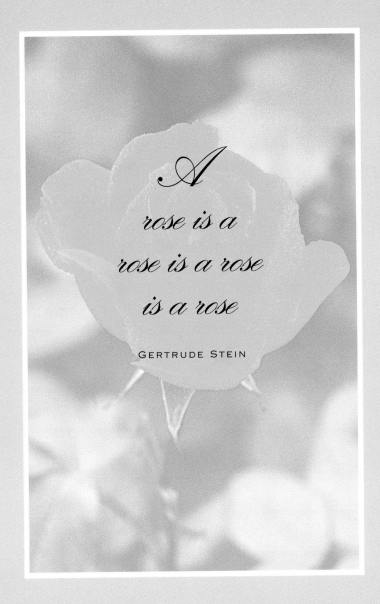

A rose is a rose is a rose is a rose

GERTRUDE STEIN

*I*f the rose puzzled its mind over the question how
it grew, it would not have been the miracle that it is.

J.B. YEATS (1871–1957)
Letters to His Son, W.B. Yeats and Others

As The Rose Grows

Yet, O thou beautiful Rose!

Queen Rose so fair and sweet,

What were lover or crown to thee

Without the clay at thy feet?

JULIA C.R. DORR

The Cultured Rose

Brought from the woods the honeysuckle twines
Around the porch, and seems, in that trim place,
A plant no longer wild; the cultured rose
There blossoms, strong in health, and will be soon
Roof-high; the wild pink crowns the garden-wall,
And with the flowers are intermingled stones
Sparry and bright, rough scatterings of the hills.

WILLIAM WORDSWORTH
(1770–1850)
The Excursion

$\mathcal{I}$T NEVER WILL RAIN ROSES:

WHEN WE WANT

TO HAVE MORE ROSES WE

MUST PLANT MORE TREES.

GEORGE ELIOT
(1819–80)
The Spanish Gypsy

Climbing
Roses

Vine, vine and eglantine,

Clasp her window,

   trail and twine!

Rose, rose and clemantis,

Trail and twine and

   clasp and kiss,

Kiss, kiss; and make her

   a bower

All of flowers, and drop

   me a flower,

Drop me a flower.

Lord Alfred Tennyson
(1845–1909)
The Window

It was the sweetest, most mysterious-looking place anyone could imagine. The high walls which shut it in were covered with the leafless stems of climbing roses, which were so thick that they were matted together. Mary Lennox knew they were roses because she had seen a great many in India. All the ground was covered with grass of wintery brown, and out of it grew clumps of bushes which were surely rose bushes if they were alive. There were numbers of standard roses which had so spread their branches that they were like little trees. There were other trees in the garden, and one of the things which made the place look strangest and lovliest was that climbing roses had run all over them and swung down in long tendrils which made light swaying curtains, and here and there they had caught at each other or at a far-reaching branch and had crept from one tree to another and made lovely bridges of themselves. There were neither leaves nor roses on them now, and Mary did not know whether they were dead or alive, but their thin grey or brown branches and sprays looked like a sort of hazy mantle spreading over everything, walls and trees, and even brown grass, where they had fallen from their fastenings and run along the ground. It was this hazy tangle from tree to tree which made it all look so mysterious.

FRANCES E. HODGSON BURNETT
(1849–1924)
The Secret Garden

THE ROSE AWAKENS —
A CELEBRATION OF LIFE

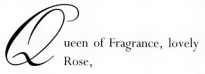

*Q*ueen of Fragrance, lovely
Rose,

The Beauties of thy Leaves disclose!

The Winter's past, the Tempests fly,

Soft Gales breathe gently thro' the Sky;

The Lark sweet warbling on the Wing

Salutes the gay return of Spring:

The silver Dews, the vernal Show'rs,

Call forth a blooming Waste of Flow'rs;

The joyous Fields, the shady Woods,

Are cloath'd with Green, or swell

with Buds;

Then haste thy Beauties to disclose,

Queen of Fragrance, lovely Rose!

WILLIAM BROOME

(1698–1745)

The Rose-Bud: To the Lady Jane Wharton

*F*ain would my Muse the
flowery treasure sing

And humble glories of the youthful
Spring;

Where opening roses breathing
sweets diffuse,

And soft carnations shower their
balmy dews;

Where lilies smile in virgin robes
of white,

The thin undress of superficial light,

And varied tulips show so dazzling gay,

Blushing bright in diversities of day.

ALEXANDER POPE
(1688–1744)
The Garden

The fateful slumber floats and flows

About the tangle of the rose;

But lo! The fated hand and heart

To rend the slumbrous curse apart!

WILLIAM MORRIS

(1834–96)

For the Briar Rose

O treacherous scent, O thorny sight,

O tangle of world's wrong and right,

What art thou 'gainst my armour's gleam

But dusky cobwebs of a dream?

WILLIAM MORRIS

(1834–96)

Another for the Briar Rose

Beautiful Sleeping Brier Rose

...Soon a brier hedge began to grow all around the castle, and it grew higher each year. Eventually it surrounded and covered the entire castle, so that it was no longer visible ... in the castle, so country folk said, was a remarkably beautiful princess they called Sleeping Brier Rose who was cursed as child and destined to sleep for a hundred years.

Many young men over the years had attempted to enter the castle and to claim this beauty for themselves only to perish on the thorns ... When the prince approached the brier hedge, he found nothing but beautiful flowers that opened of their own accord to let him through ... he found the door to the small room in which Brier Rose was asleep. There she lay, and her beauty was so marvelous that he could not take his eyes off her. Then he leaned over and gave her a kiss, and when his lips touched hers, Brier Rose opened her eyes.

The wedding of the prince with Brier Rose was celebrated in great splendour, and they lived happily to the end of their days.

THE BROTHERS GRIMM
(JAKOB LUDWIG CARL 1785–1863 &
WILLHELM CARL 1786–1859)

I CANNOT SEE WHAT FLOWERS ARE AT MY FEET,

NOR WHAT SWEET INCENSE HANGS UPON THE BOUGHS,

BUT, IN EMBALMED DARKNESS, GUESSS EACH SWEET

WHEREWITH THE SEASONABLE MONTH ENDOWS

THE GRASS, THE THICKET, AND THE FRUIT-TREE WILD;

WHITE HAWTHORN AND PASTORAL EGLANTINE;

FAST FADING VIOLETS COVER'D UP IN LEAVES;

AND MID-MAY'S ELDEST CHILD,

THE COMING MUSK-ROSE, FULL OF DEWY WINE,

THE MURNUROUS HAUNT OF FLIES ON SUMMER EVES.

JOHN KEATS
(1795–1821)
Ode to a Nightingale

Summer

HEADY-SCENTED PASSION

The world is a rose; smell it and pass it to your friends.
Persian Proverb

How wide the leaves,

Extended to their utmost, of this rose,

Whose lowest step embosoms such a space

Of ample radiance! Yet, nor amplitude

Nor height impeded, but my view with ease

Took in the full dimensions of that joy.

Near or remote, what there avails, where God

Immediate rules, and Nature, awed, suspends

Her sway? Into the yellow of the rose

Perennial, which in bright expansiveness

Lays forth its gradual blooming, redolent

Of praises to the never-wintering sun

As one, who fain would speak yet holds his peace,

Beatrice led me ...

DANTE ALIGHIERI
(1265–1321)
The Divine Comedy

*S*oon, trembling in her soft and chilly nest,

In sort of wakeful swoon, perplex'd she lay,

Until the poppied warmth of sleep oppress'd

Her soothed limbs, and soul fatigued away;

Flown, like thought, until the morrow-day;

Blissfully haven'd both from joy and pain;

Clasp'd like a missal where swart Paynims pray;

Blinded alike from sunshine and from rain,

As though a rose should shut, and be a bud again.

JOHN KEATS
(1795–1821)
The Eve of St Agnes

*I*t was very still. The tree was tall and straggling. It had thrown its briers over a hawthorn-bush, and its long streamers trailed thick, right down to the grass, splashing the darkness everywhere with great split stars, pure white. In bosses of ivory and in large splashing stars the roses gleamed on the darkness of foliage and stems of grass. Paul and Miriam stood close together, silent, and watched. Point after point the steady roses shone out to them, seeming to kindle something in their souls. The dusk came like smoke around, and still did not put out the roses.

D. H. LAWRENCE
(1885–1930)
Sons and Lovers

'Tis the last rose of summer,
Left blooming alone;
All her lovely companions
Are faded and gone;
No flower of her kindred,
No rosebush is nigh,
To reflect back her blushes,
Or give sigh for sigh.

I'll not leave thee, thou lone one,
To pine on the stem;
Since the lovely are sleeping,
Go sleep thou with them.
Thus kindly I scatter
Thy leaves o'er the bed
Where thy mates of the garden
Lie scentless and dead.

So soon may I follow,
When friendship's decay,
And from love's shining circle
The gems drop away!
When true hearts lie withered,
And fond ones are flown,
Oh! who would inhabit
This bleak world alone?

THOMAS MOORE
(1779–1852)
'Tis the last Rose of Summer

Far off she felt the red rose at her lips,

And thrilled the thorn's blood to her finger tips;

The slow sap tingling through the veiny leaf;

The gold grain climbing to the shiny sheaf,—

The breath and death of lilies — these she knew ...

FRANK L. STANTON

(1857-1927)

OCTOBER

Autumn

SWEET MEMORIES
OF ROSES FADED

Time brings roses.
Portuguese Proverb

Music, when soft voices die,

Vibrates in the memory —

Odours, when sweet violets sicken,

Live within the sense they quicken.

Rose leaves, when the rose is dead,

Are heaped for the beloved's bed;

And so thy thoughts, when thou art gone,

Love itseslf shall slumber on.

PERCY BYSSHE SHELLEY

(1792–1822)

Music, When Soft Voices Die

ROSE, ON THIS TERRACE FIFTY YEARS AGO,

WHEN I WAS IN MY JUNE, YOU IN YOUR MAY,

TWO WORDS, '*MY* ROSE' SET ALL YOUR FACE AGLOW,

AND NOW THAT I AM WHITE AND YOU ARE GRAY,

THAT BLUSH OF FIFTY YEARS AGO, MY DEAR,

BLOOMS IN THE PAST, BUT CLOSE TO ME TODAY

AS THIS RED ROSE, WHICH ON OUR TERRACE HERE

GLOWS IN THE BLUE OF FIFTY MILES AWAY.

ALFRED, LORD TENNYSON
(1809–92)
The Roses on the Terrace

From the thorn-bush comes

forth the rose.

Winter

THE BITTER THORN

THE NIGHTINGALE AND THE ROSE

… She sang first of the birth of love in the heart of a boy and a girl. And on the top-most spray of the Rose-tree there blossomed a marvellous rose, petal following petal, as song followed song. Pale was it, at first, as the mist that hangs over the river — pale as the feet of the morning, and silver as the wings of dawn. As the shadow of a rose in a mirror of silver, as the shadow of a rose in a water-pool, so was the rose that blossomed on the topmost spray of the Tree.

But the Tree cried to the Nightingale to press closer against the thorn. 'Press closer, little Nightingale', cried the Tree, 'or the Day will come before the rose is finished'.

So the Nightingale pressed closer against the thorn, and louder and louder grew her song, for she sang of the birth of passion in the soul of man and maid.

And a delicate flush of pink came into the leaves of the rose, like the flush in the face of the bridegroom when he kisses the lips of the bride. But the thorn had not yet reached her heart, so the rose's heart remained white, for only a Nightingale's heart's-blood can crimson the heart of a rose.

And the Tree cried to the Nightinglae to press closer against the thorn. 'Press closer, little Nightingale', cried the Tree 'or the Day will come before the rose is finished'.

So the Nightingale pressed closer against the thorn, and the thorn touched her heart, and a fierce pang of pain shot through her. Bitter, bitter was the pain, and wilder and wilder grew her song, for she sang of the Love that is perfected by Death, of the Love that dies not in the tomb.

OSCAR WILDE

(1854–1900)

The Nightingale and the Rose

THE ROSE IS
WEEPING FOR HER LOVE,
THE NIGHTINGALE;

AND HE IS FLYING
FAST ABOVE,

TO HER HE WILL
NOT FAIL.

ALREADY GOLDEN
EVE APPEARS;

HE WINGS HIS
WAY ALONG;

AH! LOOK HE COMES
TO KISS HER TEARS,

AND SOOTHE HER
WITH HIS SONG.

PHILIP JAMES BAILEY
(1816–1902)
'Helen's Song' *Festu*

Go, lovely Rose!

Tell her that wastes her time and me,

That now she knows,

When I resemble her to thee,

How sweet and fair she seems to be.

Tell her that's young,

And shuns to have her graces spied,

That hadst thou sprung

In desserts, where no man abide,

Thou must have uncommended died.

Small is the worth

Of beauty from the light retired;

Bid her come forth,

Suffer herself to be desired,

And not blush so to be admired.

Then die! that she

The common fate of all things rare

May read in thee;

How small a part of time they share

That are so wonderous sweet and fair!

EDMUND WALLER

(1606–87)

Go, Lovely Rose

THE LANGUAGE OF ROSES

The rose, as we know, has long been a generic symbol of love, but each bloom is said to carry a special message from the giver.

From times when courting was overseen by a chaperone and young lovers were rarely allowed a precious moment alone for private intimacies, each flower in a posy assumed a special meaning. Spare a thought for your choice of roses and hark to the message of roses you receive.

Austrian Rose: YOU ARE ALL THAT IS LOVELY

Boule de Neige Rose: JUST FOR YOU

Burgundy Rose: UNPRETENTIOUS BEAUTY

Cabbage Rose: AN AMBASSADOR

China Rose: BEAUTY ALWAYS NEW

Christmas Rose: RELIEVE MY ANXIETY

I never want the Christmas rose
    To come before its time;
The seasons, each as God bestows,
    Are simple and sublime.
I love to see the snowstorm hing:
    'Tis but the winter garb of spring.

JOHN CLARE
(1793–1864)
The Winter's Spring.

Daily Rose: I WISH YOUR SMILES
WERE FOR ME

Deep Red Rose: EMBARRASSMENT,
TIMIDNESS AND SHAME

Dog Rose: PLEASURE CAN BE MIXED
WITH PAIN

Gloire de Dijon Rose: LOVE'S MESSENGER

So home I went, but could not sleep for joy,

Reading her perfect features in the gloom,

Kissing the rose she gave me o'er and o'er,

And shaping faithful record of the glance

That graced the giving —

LORD ALFRED TENNYSON
(1809–92)
The Gardener's Daughter

John Hopper Rose: ENCOURAGEMENT

The rose is fairest when 'tis budding new,

And hope is brightest when it dawns from fears,

The rose is sweetest washed in morning dew,

And love is loveliest when embalmed in tears.

O wilding rose, whom fancy thus endears,

I bid your blossoms in my bonnet wave,

Emblem of hope and love through future years.

SIR WALTER SCOTT
(1771–1832)
The Lady of the Lake

Moss Rosebud: A CONFESSION OF LOVE

The angel of the flowers one day,

Beneath a rose-tree sleeping lay, —

That spirit whose charge 't is given

To bathe young buds in dews of heaven.

Awakening from his light repose,

The Angel whispered to the rose:

'O fondest object of my care,

Still fairest found, where all are fair;

For the sweet shade thou giv'st to me

Ask what thou wilt, 'tis granted thee.'

'Then,' said the rose, with deepening glow,

'On me another grace bestow.'

The spirit paused, in silent thought,

What grace was there that flower had not?

'Twas but a moment, — o'er the rose

A veil of moss the angel throws,

And, robed in nature's simplest weed,

Could there a flower that rose exceed?

F.A. KRUMMACHER

The Moss Rose

(Anon. translation from the German)

La France Rose. MEET ME BY MOONLIGHT

The moon in pearly light may steep
The still blue air;
The rose hath ceas'd to droop and weep,
For lo! her love is there;
He sings to her, and o'er the trees
She hears his sweet notes swim;
The world may weary, she but sees
Her love, and hears but him.

PHILIP JAMES BAILEY
(1816–1902)
'Helen's Song' *Festus*

An Overworked Moon.

Musk Rose. CAPRICIOUS BEAUTY

As late I rambled in the happy fields,

What time the sky-lark shakes the tremelous dew

From his lush clover covert; — when anew

Adventurous knights take up their dinted shields:

I saw the sweetest flower sweet nature yields,

A fresh-blown musk-rose; 'twas the first that threw

Its sweets upon the summer: graceful it grew

As is the wand that Queen Titania wields.

And as I feasted on its fragrancy,

I thought the garden rose it far excell'd:

But when, O Wells! thy roses came to me

My sense with their deliciousness was spell'd:

Soft voices had they, that with tender plea

Whispered of peace, and truth, and friendliness

    unquell'd.

JOHN KEATS

(1795–1821)

To a Friend Who Sent Me Some Roses

Peace

Peace as a rose would blossom again in my breast;

If I had only patience, and let love free,

As a bird to its nest, my love would come to me.

AURTHUR SYMONS

(1865–1945)

The Blind Heart

Provence Rose: MY HEART IS IN FLAMES

Red Rose: LOVE

And, haply, from the nectar-breathing Rose
Extract a Blush for Love!

SAMUEL TAYLOR COLERIDGE
(1772–1834)
Songs of the Pixies

Red Rosebud: PURE AND LOVELY

Single Rose: SIMPLICITY

O my luve's like a red, red rose,
That's newly sprung in June;
O my luve's like the melodie
That's sweetly played in tune.

As fair art thou, my bonnie lass,
So deep in luve am I;
And I will luve thee still, my dear,
Till a' the seas gang dry.

Till a' the seas gang dry, my dear,
And the rocks melt wi' the sun;
And I will luve thee still, my dear,
while the sands o' life shall run.

And fare thee weel, my only luve!
And fare thee weel a while!
And I will come again my luve,
Tho' it were ten thousand mile!

ROBERT BURNS
(1759–96)

Spray of White Roses: SECRECY

The rose is the flower of Venus; and Love, in order that her sweet dishonesties might be hidden, dedicated this gift of his mother to Harpocrates, the god of silence. Hence the host hangs the rose over his friendly tables, that his guests may know that beneath it what is said will be regarded as secret.

ANON

Rosa Flos Veneris

Far off most secret and inviolate Rose,
Enfold me in my hour of hours.

WILLIAM BUTLER YEATS

The Secret Rose

Thorned Rose: LOVE IS BITTERSWEET

When the rose dies, the thorn is left behind.

OVID
(43 BC —17AD)
Ars Amamtoria

Who reaches with a clumsy hand for a rose
must not complain if the thorns scratch.

H.HEINE
(1797–1856)
Rabbi of Bacharach

Thornless Rose: LOVE'S BEGINNINGS

White and Red Roses Together: UNITY

SNOW WHITE AND ROSE RED

 Two sisters once lived in a cottage in a wood, where their mother grew two rose bushes, a white one for beautiful Snow White and a crimson one for lovely Rose Red. One midwinter they took pity on a bear that begged for shelter, and every night it slept by their fire. In spring when their gentle friend departed, it tore its coat on the door, and the girls were puzzled to see gold shining beneath its fur.

Three times that summer Snow White and Rose Red came to the rescue of a greedy dwarf, who gave them nothing in return, though he had hordes of gold and jewels hidden in the forest. One day, just after they had saved the dwarf from a mighty eagle, the bear came upon the scene. The dwarf turned on the beast in fury, but with one cuff of its paw the bear silenced him for ever. Afraid, the girls turned away, but a sweet voice called them back: the rough bearskin had fallen to reveal a handsome prince, who had suffered all winter long under the dwarf's spell.

Snow white married the prince, Rose Red married his brother, and the rose bushes bloom still in the deep wood where they first met.

THE BROTHERS GRIMM
(JAKOB LUDWIG CARL 1785—1863 &
WILLHELM CARL 1786—1859)

White Rose: I WILL PROVE MYSELF
WORTHY OF YOU

She has more love than the first white rose
That comes to comfort the thin, weak air;
Her eyes have a smile they would not lose
Though all the world should be wroth with her.

ALGERNON CHARLES SWINBURNE
(1837–1909)
Southwards

White Rosebud: INNOCENT OF LOVE

Cease, foolish rosebud, cease unfolding
So fast thy bosom's unguarded sweetness!
Thy charm was a most rich withholding;
Thy beauty a perfect incompleteness

SIR WILLIAM WATSON
(1858–1935)
Cease, Foolish Rosebud

Wreath or Crown of Roses:
A REWARD FOR VIRTUE

LET US FILL OURSELVES WITH COSTLY WINE AND OINTMENTS: AND LET NO
FLOWER OF SPRING PASS BY US: LET US CROWN OURSELVES WITH ROSEBUDS,
BEFORE THEY BE WITHERED: LET NONE OF US GO WITHOUT HIS PART OF OUR
VOLUPTUOUSNESS: LET US LEAVE TOKENS OF OUR JOYFULNESS IN EVERY
PLACE, FOR THIS IS OUR PORTION, AND OUR LOT IT IS.

Apocrypha
'Wisdon of Solomon'

At ev'ry Turn, she made a
little Stand,

And thrust among the Thorns
her Lilly Hand

To draw the Rose, and ev'ry
Rose she drew

She shook the Stalk, and brush'd
away the Dew:

Then party-colour'd Flow'rs of
white and red

She wove, to make a Garland
for her Head ...

JOHN DRYDEN
(1631–1700)
Palamon and Arcite

64

*S*he wore a wreath of roses
 The night that we first met;
Her lovely face was smiling
 Beneath her curls of jet.
Her footsteps had the lightness,
 Her voice the joyous tone —
The tokens of a youthful heart,
 Where sorrow is unknown.
I saw her but a moment,
 Yet methinks I see her now,
With the wreath of summer flowers
 Upon her snowy brow.

THOMAS H. BAYLY
(1797–1839)
She Wore a Wreath of Roses

Yellow Rose: JEALOUSY

ROSES TO THE TABLE

Just a few of the roses we gathered from the Isar
Are fallen, and their mauve-red petals on the cloth
Float like boats on a river, while other
Roses are ready to fall, reluctant and loth.

She laughs at me across the table saying
I am beautiful. I look at the rumpled young roses
And suddenly realise, in them as in me,
How lovely is the self this day discloses.

D. H. LAWRENCE
(1885–1930)
Roses on the Breakfast Table

Rose-hip Tea

The sweets of sense,

Do they not oft with kind accession flow,

To raise harmonious fancy's native charm?

So, while we taste the fragrance of the rose,

Glows not her blush the fairer?

MARK ARKENSIDE

The Pleasures of the Imagination

The ripe fruits (hips) of wild roses are harvested, dried and shredded to make the tea. Use one teaspoonful for each cup, pour boiling water over it, allow to infuse, then strain.

This delightful beverage is an excellent source of vitamin C as well as vitamins A, E and B. It can be taken hot in winter with a slice of lemon, a little honey and a pinch of spice, or iced in summer with sprigs of mint, or peppermint, honey, ice cubes and lemon slices. Hibiscus flowers are often blended with rose-hip tea for "fragrant enjoyment".

JOHN & ROSEMARY HEMPHILL

Hemphill's Book of Herbs

LANSDOWNE PUBLISHING, AUSTRALIA, 1990

Rose Petal Sandwiches

Makes about 9 fingers

CHOOSE FRAGRANT ROSES IN SEASON. ALLOW TWO MEDIUM ROSES FOR EACH SANDWICH. BE SURE TO USE PETALS THAT HAVE NOT BEEN SPRAYED WITH PESTICIDE, AND REMOVE THE WHITE TRIANGULAR HEEL FROM THE BASE.

4 oz / 125 g unsalted butter, softened

a few drops rosewater

1–2 teaspoons icing (powdered) sugar, or to taste

9 slices of pre-sliced white bread

6 medium roses, washed and dried

Lightly whip butter with rosewater and confectioners' sugar.
For each sandwich, spread three slices of bread with butter. Stack slices together, trim crusts, and cut into 3 even fingers. Fill the 2 layers of each finger with petals, letting them overflow the edges slightly so that the petals show. Decorate the plate with extra rose petals.

SHERIDAN ROGERS

Entertaining at Home

LANSDOWNE PUBLISHING, AUSTRALIA, 1994

Rose Salad

On a bed of mescalin or some of the larger herb leaves arrange your chosen edible flowers: nasturtium flowers, honeyed bergamot flowers and leaf sprigs, sky blue borage flowers, purple violets, pink or red rose petals and dill or fennel flowers.

In eating flowers we partake of the more refined essences of the plant, the final stage before returning to seed and completing the circle of plant life. So the flower offers a more subtle energy, as well as sweet nectar ... flowers can speak to us and contain special healing powers. To gather and make this salad is one way of being with flowers and learning how they express the harmony of nature.

JEANNE ROSE
Herbal Guide to Inner Health
GROSSET AND DUNLAP, NEW YORK.

Rose Petal Bowl

Use either cold boiled water or still mineral water so that the ice does not become cloudy, and chose two glass or metal bowls sized so that one sits inside the other with at least a 1-inch (2.5-cm) gap in between.

Pour about 1 cup of water and a handful of petals into the larger bowl, sit the smaller bowl inside, and weigh down with a heavy pan or other weight, then freeze. Once frozen, add another cup of water and petals to the bowl and freeze again. Continue this process until the bowl is full. To do so, step-by-step, ensures an even spacing of petals throughout the bowl.

When completely frozen, carefully remove inner bowl. If removal is difficult, fill it quickly with hot water and drain. Remove the outer bowl, dipping in hot water if necessary. Return the ice bowl to the freezer until it is to be brought to the table. Place on a platter, surround with fruit of the season and fill with dessert or refreshment.

Chocolate Rose Leaves

Select unblemished rose leaves, wash and dry thoroughly. Melt chocolate in a bowl over hot water. Using melted chocolate and a paint brush, carefully and evenly coat the underside of each leaf with chocolate. Take care not to get any chocolate on the tops of the leaves or they will be very difficult to separate.

When set, add a second coat. Place on non-stick parchment (baking paper), chocolate facing upwards, and put in the refrigerator or in a cool place until set hard . When required, carefully peel the rose leaves away from the chocolate. Chocolate rose leaves are a delightful finishing touch to any sweet dish. Chocolate Pears and Rose Leaves pictured.

Crystallised Rose Petals

1 egg white
confectioner's (icing) sugar, sifted
red or pink roses

Line a tray with parchment (baking paper). Whip the egg white until frothy but not stiff. Dip rose petals or whole roses into the egg white, allowing any excess to drip away. Dip into the sugar and shake gently to remove any excess. Place on a tray to dry overnight.

Tender, succulent and appealing, the addition of cryst-allised rose petals makes a sweet dish a delicacy.

Musk Rose Water

Take two handfuls of your Musk Rose leaves, put them into about a quart of fair water and a quarter pound of sugar, let this stand and steep about half and hour, then take your water and flowers and pour them out of one vessel into another till such time as the water hath taken the scent and taste of the flowers, then set it in a cool place a-cooling and you will find it a most excellent scent-water.

WILLIAM RABISHA
The Whole Body of Cookery Dissected
1675

The rose looks fair, but fairer we it deem
For that sweet odour which doth in it live.

WILLIAM SHAKESPEARE
(1564–1616)

The Aromatic Rose

Rose Water

O royal Rose! the Roman dress'd
His feast with thee; thy petal press'd
Augustan brows; thine odour fine,
Mix'd with the three-times-mingled wine,
Lent the long Thracian draught its zest.

AUSTIN DOBSON
To a June Rose

Rose Essential Oil

But earthlier happy is the rose distill'd,
Than that which withering on the Virgin thorn
Grows, lives, and dies, in single blessedness.

WILLIAM SHAKESPEARE
(1564–1616)
A Midsummer-Night's Dream

 As the rose is "queen of all flowers", rose oil has been named the "queen of essential oils". The petals of thirty damask roses produce just one drop of precious *Rose otto* essential oil.

Rose oil is probably best loved for its marvellously feminine and sensual fragrance. As the poets attest, it has been the aphrodisiac of the ages. But rose oil is valued as highly for its therapeutic qualities and can be used, diluted, via face and body massage, skin care, or vaporisers to treat nervousness, sadness or long term stress. Refreshing in baths, with a mild tonic affect on sensitive skin, rose oil is generally balancing and an excellent remedy for female disorders as well as digestive maladies.

A LEGEND TELLS OF JEHANGIR, THE MOGUL PRINCE,
WHO ORDERED ROSES TO BE FLOATED IN EVERY
CANAL RUNNING THROUGH THE ROYAL GARDENS TO
CELEBRATE HIS WEDDING. HIS BEAUTIFUL WIFE,
WHILE RUNNING HER FINGERS THROUGH THE SCENTED
WATER, WAS DELIGHTED TO FIND THAT A FRAGRANT
OIL CLUNG TO HER HANDS. HER DOTING HUSBAND
HAD IT BOTTLED AS A TRIBUTE TO HER.

"To Make Oyle of Roses — Take of oyle eighteen ounces, the buds of Roses (the white ends of them cut away) three ounces, lay the Roses abroad in the shadow four and twenty houres, then put them in a glass to the oyle, and stop the glass close, and set it in the sunne for at least forty days."

JOHN PARTRIDGE
1586
The Treasurie of Hidden Secrets and Commodious Conceits

Enhancing Potpourri Blends

MEDITATION AND TRANQUILLITY:

bergamot, lavender, rose, sandalwood, patchouli, ylang ylang, jasmine.

DEVOTIONAL:

neroli, rose, ylang ylang, boronia, jasmine.

HEALING:

bay, rose, sandalwood, wintergreen, mandarin.

WEDDINGS AND FESTIVITIES:

neroli, rose, boronia, jasmine.

FEMININITY:

bergamot, rose-geranium, lavender, rose, jasmine.

FOR SOOTHING SLEEP:

lavender, valerian, rose, lemon-verbena.

There will I make thee beds of roses

And a thousand fragrant posies

A cap of flowers, and a kirtle

Embroidered all with leaves of myrtle.

CHRISTOPHER MARLOWE

(1564–93)

Come live with me and be my Love

Potpourri

4 cups dried flowers and leaves
1 tablespoon orris powder
1 teaspoon ground cinnamon
1 teaspoon each essential oil you have chosen

Gather flowers and leaves in dry weather early in the day, before the sun has become too hot. Perfumed roses, especially red and pink ones can be mixed with other fragrant flowers from your garden, lavender, citrus blossoms, jasmine, lemon verbena and scented-leaved geraniums are all suitable. Spread your harvest out on racks of paper in a shady, airy place to dry.

When crisp-dry, measure the flowers and leaves (large leaves should be crunched into smaller pieces) and put them into a covered earthenware or glass container.

Mix orris powder and cinnamon, then add the oils and blend well. Sprinkle this crumbly mixture over the potpourri, stir well, cover and leave for 2–3 weeks, stirring occasionally. The blend is now ready to be placed in decorative bowls. Pieces of cinnamon bark, whole cloves, bay leaves and dried strips of orange or lemon peel are also excellent additions to the potpourri mixture.

JOHN & ROSEMARY HEMPHILL
Hemphill's Book of Herbs
LANSDOWNE PUBLISHING, AUSTRALIA, 1990

Live all thy sweet life thro',
Sweet Rose, dew-sprent,
Drop down thy evening dew
To gather it anew
When day is bright:
I fancy thou was meant
Chiefly to give delight.

CHRISTINA ROSSETTI
(1830–94)
A Summer Wish

Published by Lansdowne Publishing Pty Ltd
Level 5, 70 George Street, Sydney NSW 2000, Australia

First Published in 1995
Reprinted 1996

© Copyright Lansdowne Publishing Pty Ltd 1995
© Copyright design: Lansdowne Publishing Pty Ltd 1995

Managing Director Jane Curry
Publishing Manager: Deborah Nixon
Production Manager: Sally Stokes
Project Coordinator/Editor: Bronwyn Hilton
Compiled by Bronwyn Hilton
Designer: Kathie Baxter Smith

Printed in Singapore by Tien Wah Press (Pte) Ltd

National Library of Australia Cataloguing-in-Publication data:
A gift book of roses

ISBN 1 86302 416 6
1. Roses - Literary collections. I. Hilton, Bronwyn. 1968- .
820.8036